HEINEMANN ELT GUIDED READERS

ELEMENTARY LEVEL

KV-042-050

RODERICK NEILSEN

The Official

THE SIXTH FORM CENTRE
BROOKE HOUSE
LEARNING RESOURCES

LOCATION: Library

COLLECTION: Reader

CLASSMARK: NEI

BARCODE No: 512780

DATE: 17|10|2003.

HEINEMANN ELT

Brooke House College

ELEMENTARY LEVEL

Series Editor: John Milne

The Heinemann ELT Guided Readers provide a choice of enjoyable reading material for learners of English. The series is published at five levels – Starter, Beginner, Elementary, Intermediate and Upper. At **Elementary Level**, the control of content and language has the following main features:

Information Control

Stories have straightforward plots and a restricted number of main characters. Information which is vital to the understanding of the story is clearly presented and repeated when necessary. Difficult allusion and metaphor are avoided and cultural backgrounds are made explicit.

Structure Control

Students will meet those grammatical features which they have already been taught in their elementary course of studies. Other grammatical features occasionally occur with which the students may not be so familiar, but their use is made clear through context and reinforcement. This ensures that the reading as well as being enjoyable provides a continual learning situation for the students. Sentences are kept short – a maximum of two clauses in nearly all cases – and within sentences there is a balanced use of simple adverbial and adjectival phrases. Great care is taken with pronoun reference.

Vocabulary Control

At **Elementary Level** there is a limited use of a carefully controlled vocabulary of approximately 1,100 basic words. At the same time, students are given some opportunity to meet new or unfamiliar words in contexts where their meaning is obvious. The meaning of words introduced in this way is reinforced by repetition. Help is also given to the students in the form of vivid illustrations which are closely related to the text.

Contents

The People in This Story

Polus
an immigration officer

Selina
Polus' wife

Jansh
Polus' and Selina's young son

Jay
an immigration officer

Deva
Polus' and Jay's boss

**The Chief
of Police and Immigration**

Joseph
a farmer

Myra
Joseph's wife, a healer

Lisa
Myra's niece

Saran Tuho
an illegal immigrant

1

The *Beluga*

It was a dark night. There was no moonlight. A rusty old ship came slowly into Port Luck. Its name was the *Beluga*. There were men standing on the quayside. They waited silently for the ship.

Two of the men were wearing uniforms and they had guns in their belts. Both of these men had large flash-lights in their hands. They were immigration officers. Their names were Polus and Jay.

The ship came towards the quayside. Two sailors on the ship threw ropes to the men on the quayside.

*Two of the men were wearing uniforms and
they had guns in their belts.*

A few moments later, the ship's engines stopped. Six men pushed a small footbridge towards the side of the ship. Then Polus and Jay went along the footbridge and onto the ship.

The ship's captain spoke to them.

'Good evening, officers,' he said. His mouth was dry. He was nervous.

'We are from the Immigration Department,' Polus said. 'We must inspect your ship. Do you have any passengers on board?'

'This is a cargo ship,' the captain replied. 'We have a cargo of vegetables, fruit and rice from the Zipa Islands. We don't have any passengers.'

'I'm sorry, but we must check,' Polus said. 'Take us down into the ship's hold. I want to see your cargo. Bring three of your men.'

The captain gave orders to three sailors, and Polus and Jay followed them down some stairs. In the hold there were sacks of rice, sacks of onions and sacks of potatoes. There were large wooden boxes. Jay shone his flashlight at a box and shouted to a sailor.

'Open this!' he ordered.

The sailor opened it. Inside the box there were bananas. Polus told the sailors to open more boxes. In some of the boxes there were more bananas, in other boxes there were pineapples.

'There's nobody here,' Jay said quickly. 'Let's go.' He was an impatient man.

'I'm not so sure,' Polus answered. 'We know that many

people are trying to come here from the Zipa Islands.' He shone his flashlight again. This time he saw a pile of boxes against a wall.

'Move those boxes!' Polus ordered.

'They're heavy,' one of the sailors replied nervously.

'Move them!' Polus said quickly. The sailors slowly moved the boxes. Behind the boxes, Polus saw a door.

'Open that door,' he said.

'You don't have to open that door, officer,' a voice said.

It was the captain. He put his hand in his pocket and took out some banknotes. Jay turned and shone his flashlight at the captain. There was money in the man's hand. Jay looked at Polus. Polus saw the money, too.

'Open the door,' Polus said again.

A sailor pulled the door open. There was a small room behind the door. Polus could hear sounds from the room.

'Come out!' Polus ordered.

There was silence for a minute. Then a man came out of the room. He moved slowly. Other people followed – mainly young men, but a few older men also. The illegal immigrants all moved slowly. They had been hiding in the hold of the *Beluga* for forty days.

Jay came forward. 'Hurry up!' he shouted, and pushed one man hard. The man had a thin, strong face.

'They're like rats in a hole,' Jay said.

'They're not bad people,' Polus said quietly to Jay. 'They're just unlucky.'

Jay was angry. But Polus did not notice.

'This ship may not leave Port Luck,' Polus said to the

9

captain. 'Now, everybody, go up onto the deck.'

Jay and Polus followed the group of illegal immigrants up the stairs. When they were all on the deck of the ship, the two immigration officers counted the illegals. There were thirty of them. They were all very tired and hungry. They had come a long way in a small room in the ship's hold. The illegals had given the captain all their money to come to Suba. Now the immigration officers had found them.

Suddenly there was a noise. Then a loud *splash!*

'Quick!' Jay shouted. He ran to the side of the ship. He shone his flashlight down to the water. Polus shone his flashlight, too. There was a man in the water. He was a strong swimmer. He was swimming to the shore.

'I can shoot him from here,' Jay said. He pointed his gun, but Polus put his hand on Jay's arm.

'Don't shoot,' Polus said. 'We don't want to kill him. We'll find him later.'

Jay was angry, but he put his gun away.

2

Forged Papers

The next day was Sunday. On Monday, Polus went to his office early in the morning as usual. There was a piece of paper with a handwritten message on his desk.

COME TO MY OFFICE IMMEDIATELY, the message said. The

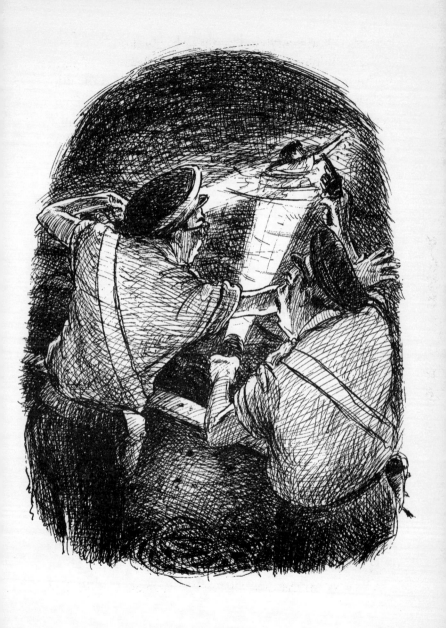

'Don't shoot,' Polus said.

handwriting was Deva's. He was Polus' boss and the Head of the Immigration Department in Port Luck.

Polus went to his boss' office. He knocked on the door and went in.

'Hello, Polus,' Deva said. 'Come in.' He smiled, but it was a cold smile. His face was tired. 'Sit down. I want to talk to you about the men that you found on the *Beluga*.'

'Yes, sir. There were thirty illegals. All from the Zipa Islands. Poor fellows. They're all in jail now. All except one. I'm afraid that one man escaped. We haven't found him yet.'

'Last night *all* the men escaped from the jail,' Deva said. He looked carefully at Polus.

There was a short silence.

'What? Escaped?' Polus said. 'How?'

'This morning the guards were all in a deep sleep. Someone helped the illegals to escape.'

'They'll go into the forest, I guess,' Polus said. 'It will be difficult to find them. It won't be impossible, but it will be difficult. And it will take time.'

'Yes, Polus,' Deva said. 'It's not easy to live in the forest. And here in Port Luck, the illegals could find work. This town is growing. New roads, new houses and factories need people to build them. There is work here.'

'That is why these men come,' Polus said.

'Yes,' Deva said. 'But there are too many of them. The government is really worried. And my boss in Ranamena telephones me every week. "What are you doing about the illegal workers?" he asks. And now every ship that comes here brings more and more men. It's getting very difficult.'

Polus and Deva were silent for a minute.

Then Deva spoke again. 'Polus, I have been doing this job for a long time – twenty-five years. Every year, the problems get worse. I've had enough. I want to go back to my village. I've decided to retire next year.'

Polus didn't answer. He didn't know what to say.

'And how is your family?' Deva asked. 'You have a wife and child, don't you?'

'Yes, sir. My son, Jansh. He's four. And my wife is going to have another baby in two or three weeks.'

Deva smiled. 'You are a good officer, Polus,' he said.

'Thank you, sir,' Polus replied.

He was surprised. 'Why is Deva saying this?' he thought.

There was a moment of silence.

Then Deva said, 'Polus, we *must* find these illegals soon. There will be trouble for us all if we don't find them soon.'

Polus got up and went back to his office. He could not think about the thirty men. He could only think about Deva.

'Deva is going to retire!' Polus thought. 'Why did he speak to me like that? Does he want me to take his job? But what about Jay? He's older than me.'

———

Some days later, Polus was in his office. There was a knock on his door. It was Rosa.

When people came into the office for work permits, Rosa checked their identity cards and other papers first. Then she took the papers to Polus or to Jay for them to sign.

'Polus, could you check these papers, please? A man came in with them. I think that something is wrong. Look at this ID card. I don't think that it's real. I think that it's forged.'

Polus looked at the papers. He saw a photo of a young man with a thin, strong face. The name on the papers was Saran Tuho.

'I've seen that face before,' Polus thought. 'But where?'

'I told him to come back tomorrow,' Rosa said.

Suddenly Polus remembered.

'The *Beluga*,' he thought. 'He was on the *Beluga*. He is the man that Jay pushed. He was the man who jumped into the sea.'

3

'That's Him!'

Later that day, Polus had finished work. He was in the town centre. Suddenly he saw two men in an old truck. One of the men was a young man with a thin, strong face.

'That's him!' Polus said to himself. 'That's Saran Tuho, the man that we're looking for!'

The old truck went along the street. It did not go very fast.

Polus stopped a taxi. He jumped in. 'Follow that truck,' he said to the taxi driver.

They followed the old truck along the road out of Port Luck.

'Don't get too close,' Polus ordered. 'I don't want the driver of the truck to see us.'

The truck turned onto another road. This road went into the forest. It was a very rough road. It was difficult for the taxi to follow.

Soon Polus could not see the old truck any more. The taxi came to a fork in the road. Left or right?

'Go left,' Polus told the taxi driver.

They drove for several minutes, but then the road came to an end in the middle of the forest. The driver turned the taxi around and drove back to the fork. This time they took the right fork. The road got rougher and rougher. The taxi driver did not want to go any further. The truck had disappeared.

'OK. Turn around and go back,' Polus ordered the taxi driver.

Suddenly the taxi started to shake. The driver stopped and got out. The taxi had a flat tyre! He got the tools out of the back of the car and started to take off the wheel. Then they heard a shout.

Polus and the driver looked up. They saw a man and a boy. The boy was about sixteen.

'What's the trouble?' the man asked.

Polus pointed to the flat tyre. 'We've got a flat tyre,' he replied.

'My son will help you,' the man said. He had a kind face. 'My name is Joseph. This is my son. He'll help your driver. Come to my house and have some tea. My house is near here.'

Polus walked along the road with Joseph. They came to a small path. At the end of the path there was a wooden house. Polus saw a rice field not far from the house. There were chickens and ducks and a dog near the house.

Joseph and Polus went inside the house. There were two women in the main room. The older woman sat in a chair near a wooden table. There were small bowls of green, red and brown powder on the table. The younger woman was painting a picture. It was a picture of a man and a woman by the sea.

'This is my wife, Myra,' Joseph said. The older woman smiled. 'And this is my niece, Lisa.'

The young woman looked up. She had pretty, bright eyes.

Then they heard a shout.

'That's a good painting,' Polus said.

'Thank you,' she said, and looked down again.

'Please sit down,' Joseph said to Polus. 'I'll bring some tea.'

Polus did not sit down at first. He looked around the room. There were more paintings on the wall. They were pictures of islands and palm trees and beaches.

'Did you paint all these?' Polus asked.

'Yes,' Lisa said.

'They are very good,' Polus said. He went closer to look at the paintings. At that moment, he saw something through the window. It was the old truck!

Joseph came in with the tea.

'We don't get many visitors here,' Joseph said. 'Why have you come to the forest?'

'I'm from the Immigration Department,' Polus answered.

There was a short cry. It was Lisa. She got up and ran out of the room.

'I'm from the Immigration Department.'

4

'I Have a Duty to Catch This Man'

Polus looked at Joseph. 'I am looking for some illegal immigrants,' he said. 'They were on a ship that arrived a few days ago. I saw one of the men today in an old grey truck. I followed the truck into the forest, but then I lost it. That truck is now behind your house.'

There was a silence. The two men looked at each other.

'Do you know where this man is?' Polus asked. He took out his notebook and Saran Tuho's ID card and he put them on the table. 'Saran Tuho is his name, I believe. If you know where he is, tell me.'

Joseph spoke quietly. 'You cannot send him back to Zipa,' he said.

'Are you from Zipa, too?' Polus asked.

'No, I am from Suba. But my wife is from the Zipa Islands. She came here to Suba many years ago.'

'And your niece, Lisa?'

'She is from the Zipa Islands,' Joseph said. 'Her parents died two years ago. A storm destroyed their house. Saran and his family helped her. Saran sent her here. He promised to follow. The immigration laws were not so strict two years ago.'

'They are becoming stricter and stricter now,' Polus thought.

'But these people are poor,' Joseph said. 'They need work. We have work here ...'

Polus agreed, but he could not say anything. His duty was to catch illegal immigrants.

At that moment, Joseph's son came into the house.

'We've changed your tyre, sir,' the boy said. 'Your driver is ready to go.'

Polus wanted to go as well. 'I don't know what to do,' he thought. 'These people are kind and gentle. But I have a duty to catch this man, Saran Tuho.'

'Is Saran hiding in the forest with the other men?' Polus asked.

Nobody answered.

'Tell him that they must come back to Port Luck,' Polus said. 'If they stay in the forest, we will have to look for them. My boss will send the police. They will have guns. We don't want to hurt anybody.'

Joseph shook his head but said nothing.

———

Polus and the taxi driver drove back to Port Luck.

'It is late,' Polus said to himself. 'I'll go home. I'll write a report for Deva tomorrow.'

He put his hand in his pocket to get his notebook. It was not there. He had left it at Joseph's house.

'I don't want Joseph and his family to get into trouble,' Polus thought. 'I think that they're good people. Perhaps the girl loves Saran Tuho. She was upset when I said, "Immigration Department". She is a good artist. Perhaps she made that ID card.'

———

Polus arrived home. His house was near the centre of Port

21

Luck. His wife, Selina, opened the door. There were tears in her eyes. She was very worried.

'What's wrong, Selina?' Polus asked.

'It's Jansh,' she said. 'We went to the beach today. You know that he likes to play on the beach. When we came back he was sick. He has a fever.'

They went immediately to their son's room. The boy was sleeping. His skin was hot.

'I've put cool towels on him, but his body is still hot,' Selina said.

'We will watch him carefully,' Polus said. 'If he's not better tomorrow, we'll get a doctor.' They went back to the living-room.

'Do you want some tea?' his wife asked.

'Yes, please,' Polus said. He sat down. He told Selina about Joseph. She listened.

'Why can't these people stay here?' Selina said when Polus had finished his story. 'Port Luck is becoming an important town. There are many jobs.'

'Yes, that's true, Selina. But there are many people in Suba, too. Our people must come first,' Polus replied.

'I hope that these men can stay, Polus,' Selina said. 'Now, I must go to bed. I am very tired.' She got up and left the room.

Polus stayed in the living-room. He was tired too but he could not sleep. Life was so difficult. He thought about his meeting with Joseph. He thought about his son. He thought about the conversation with his boss, Deva.

'I'd like to be the new Head of Immigration,' he thought. 'I would earn more money, and then I could get a bigger house for the family. We could move away from the centre of Port Luck. It would be better for Jansh and the new baby. It's so noisy and dirty here now.'

5

A Visitor

The next morning, Jansh still had a fever. He was weak, and he would not eat.

'I'll call the doctor when I get to the office,' Polus said to his wife.

Polus went to his office and phoned the doctor. The phone rang and rang but there was no answer.

Polus had to start work. He had a lot of papers to read and to sign. He began to look at them, but he could not think clearly. He was worried about his son.

'I saw you get into a taxi yesterday,' a voice said. 'What happened?'

It was Jay. Polus looked up. He did not want to tell Jay about Joseph and the house in the forest.

'Eh? Yes, I saw one of the men from the *Beluga*,' Polus replied. 'He was in an old truck. I jumped into a taxi and followed the truck, but then I lost it. I took the wrong road. Then we had a flat tyre. I was in the forest for hours.'

'There's a young woman outside,' Jay said. 'She wants to see you, Polus.'

There was a short silence.

'Tell her to come in,' Polus said. Jay went out.

A few moments later, a young woman came in. It was Lisa. She had a red silk scarf on her head. She sat down and put something on Polus' desk. It was his notebook.

'Thank you,' Polus said. 'Is that why you came?'

'I know that you are a good man. Please help us,' Lisa said.

'How can I help you?' Polus asked.

'Saran and I want to get married. He is a good man. He looked after me when my parents died. Now he is looking after his family and friends. They need work.'

'Saran came into this office with his ID and other papers yesterday, didn't he?' Polus asked. 'How did he get them?'

Lisa smiled. 'Do you think that I'm a good artist?' she asked.

'Did you make Saran's papers?' Polus asked. 'Did you forge them?'

Suddenly the phone rang. It was his wife Selina. She was crying.

A few moments later, a young woman came in.

'Polus, Jansh is worse! His face is white, like a ghost. He is very ill.'

'I'll go and get the doctor at his office now,' Polus said.

'Oh, please hurry, Polus,' Selina cried. She put the phone down.

'What is wrong?' Lisa asked.

'My son is very ill. I have to go and find a doctor.'

'My aunt – Aunt Myra – is a great healer,' Lisa said. 'She can help your son.'

'Thank you,' Polus replied. 'But I can't … I can't accept your help. I have to go now. Tell Saran Tuho and his men to come to Port Luck. I have not written a report about them yet. I will wait a little longer, but not too long.'

There were tears in Lisa's eyes. She got up and left without another word. Polus could only think of his son.

Jay came into Polus' office a few seconds later.

'Who was that girl?' he asked.

'She needs a new ID card. That's all,' Polus said.

Jay looked at him.

'I have to go to find the doctor now,' said Polus. 'My son —'

He picked up his notebook quickly and left his office. Something fell to the floor. Polus did not notice it. But Jay did.

He picked it up. It was a piece of paper. He read:

6

Aunt Myra

Polus went into the street. 'Doctors never come when you ask them,' he thought. 'They're always too busy.'

He stopped a taxi and got in. He did not see that Jay was watching him from a window. Jay went into the street. He stopped another taxi and followed Polus.

————

Selina was crying. She was with Jansh.

'Oh, where is the doctor?' she thought. 'And where is Polus?' It was nearly midday.

Then she heard a knock on the front door. She went to the door and opened it. Two women stood outside. The older woman spoke first.

'My name is Myra. This is my niece, Lisa. Your son is ill.'

'That is true. But who are you? How do you know that Jansh is ill?' Selina asked in surprise.

'We can explain later,' Lisa said. 'My aunt knows a lot about healing. May we see your son?'

Selina was very surprised, but Myra had a wise and kind face. Perhaps it would be all right.

'Come in,' she said. The women followed her to Jansh's room.

'How long has he been like this?' Myra asked when she saw the boy.

'Two days ago we went to the beach,' Selina replied.

'We often go to the beach in the afternoon. When we came home, Jansh was sick. He has a fever now and he won't eat.'

Myra said nothing. She pulled back the bedsheet and lifted one of the little boy's feet. She looked between his toes.

'What are you looking for?' asked Selina.

'A little mark – here, look,' Myra said. She held two of the boy's toes apart. 'A siren crab bit him. They are rare here in Suba but I come from the Zipa Islands. Siren crabs are common there. They are small but very poisonous. The crab's poison works slowly and sometimes people die. Now, get me some hot water, please.'

Selina went to the kitchen and heated some water on the stove. When the water was hot, Selina put it in a bowl and took it to Myra. Myra took a small jar of red powder from her bag. She poured some of the red powder into the water. Gently, Myra lifted Jansh's head.

'Here, little one. Drink this,' Myra said. The boy drank a little, then he put his head down again.

'Your husband told Lisa about your son. That is why we came,' Myra said.

'Polus sent you?' Selina asked in surprise.

'No,' Lisa replied. 'He didn't want our help.'

'Why didn't he want your help?' Selina asked.

'Yesterday he went to our house,' Lisa said. 'He left his notebook. Your address was in the notebook.

'I went to his office to give him the notebook,' Lisa went on. 'I then asked your husband for help. We have

'A siren crab bit him.'

friends who came here from the Zipa Islands. They hid on a ship. We don't want them to go back to the Zipa Islands. They are poor. They have no work on the islands.'

'Polus told me about these people,' Selina said. 'But how can he help you?'

'Our friends need work papers,' Lisa said.

'Polus can't help them,' Selina said. 'They are illegal immigrants.'

'He can help them,' Lisa said. 'I'm an artist. I can make the papers. Most people can't see that the papers are not real. But we need the official stamp.'

'Polus can't do what you ask,' Selina said. 'He has to stop illegal immigrants coming to Suba.'

'Perhaps you're right,' Myra said, and smiled sadly. She looked at Jansh. 'Your little boy will sleep for many hours. But he'll be stronger tomorrow.'

Then the front door opened and Polus came in.

7

The Watcher

Jay sat in the taxi and watched Polus go into his home.

There was an old car outside the house. Jay went to look at it. He saw a red scarf on the seat. He remembered the girl at the Immigration office. She had worn a red scarf on her head.

Then the front door of Polus' house opened again. Jay

went back to the taxi. Two women came out of the house and they got into the car. One of them was the young woman who had come to the Immigration office.

'So Polus is helping these people!' Jay said to himself. He got back into the taxi. 'I'll follow them.'

Jay followed the old car out of Port Luck and into the forest.

'Is this where Polus came yesterday?' Jay thought. 'Who or what is Polus hiding? Deva will be interested in this.'

After some time, the old car turned off the rough track.

'Stop here,' Jay ordered the taxi driver.

Jay got out of the taxi. He soon found the path and then he saw a house. Near the house was the old car. The two women had got out.

The older woman went into the house. A young man came out of the house and spoke to the young woman. Jay knew his face. It was the illegal that he had pushed on the *Beluga*! Jay put his hand on his gun.

'So this young woman is helping illegal immigrants,' Jay thought. 'Does Polus know where they are? Why hasn't he made a report? Everybody thinks that Polus is honest. But this young woman came to the office. She left a message in Polus' notebook. She probably left some money as well. Then she went to Polus' house. Is Polus helping illegal immigrants, too? This is interesting.'

Jay moved forward a little. But his foot stepped on a dry branch. There was a sharp noise – *crack!* The branch broke. The young man and woman turned their heads and looked at Jay. The woman shouted, 'Run, Saran!' The man began to run away towards the forest.

Jay was angry. He took out his gun and shouted, 'Stop!'

Suddenly something hard and sharp hit him on the side of his head. He fell to the ground. For a few moments he saw and heard nothing. At last he stood up and looked towards the forest. The illegal had disappeared.

Jay looked around. The young woman was standing about twenty metres away. She had a catapult in her hands. Jay ran towards her.

'You did that!' he said. 'You – you —' His face was red. He grabbed her arm. 'Come with me!' he shouted.

He pulled Lisa towards the house. He had his gun in one hand as he pushed open the front door.

Joseph and Myra were inside.

'Don't move!' Jay shouted.

'Don't hurt her,' Joseph said quietly.

'You are protecting illegal immigrants!' Jay shouted.

'Don't hurt her,' Joseph said again.

'You will all go to prison for this!' Jay shouted. But he let go of Lisa's arm. He looked round the room.

'I can bring the police to find those men,' Jay said. 'You'll all go to prison. Or perhaps you would like to give me something?'

'We are poor farmers,' Joseph said sadly. 'We really have nothing to give you.'

'I saw some sacks of rice outside. Take them to my car. You can find more things to give me later,' Jay said.

Lisa was angry. 'You are taking things from my aunt and uncle!' she cried.

*Suddenly something hard and sharp hit him
on the side of his head.*

Jay smiled at her. His face was still ugly and red.

'Do you want them to go to prison instead? Prison life is very hard. I will come back tomorrow. Find some money for me by then.'

8

Blackmail

It was Saturday morning, the day after Myra's visit. Polus did not have to go to work. He got up and went into his son's room. Jansh was still in bed. But his eyes were open and he smiled. His mother came in.

'Jansh is much better!' Selina said. 'He has eaten something at last. Aren't you glad, Polus?'

'Of course I'm glad. But I'm worried. We have accepted help from Myra. The illegal immigrants are her friends. I know where they are, but I haven't told Deva. I haven't done my duty,' Polus said.

'Does it matter? Our son was dying and all the doctors were busy. Myra saved Jansh's life!'

Polus looked sad. 'Lisa brought my notebook back,' he said to his wife. 'When I opened it, I found some money inside.'

'But Polus,' his wife replied. 'We are not rich. Soon we will have another child. We need more money. Keep it. Nobody will know.'

Later that morning, Polus went to the shops. It was a hot day. He decided to buy a cold drink. He went to a coffee shop. He had a lemonade and read the newspaper.

Suddenly a shadow came across his newspaper. He looked up. It was Jay. Polus did not want to talk, but Jay sat down. Jay had a smile on his face, but it was not a friendly smile.

'Hello, Polus. How's your son?' Jay asked.

'He's better, thank you, Jay,' Polus answered.

'That's good. And your wife is going to have another child soon, isn't she? Children are expensive. It is lucky that you have a good job.'

Jay laughed. He ordered a coffee, then he spoke to Polus again. 'Do you remember those men that we found on the *Beluga*?'

'Yes.'

'I saw one of them yesterday. The man who jumped from the ship.'

'Where did you see him?' Polus asked. He was surprised.

'At a house in the forest. I think that you know the place,' Jay said.

Polus was afraid. But he said nothing at first. 'What happened?' he asked.

'Do you remember the girl who came to see you yesterday? I followed her to your house. Then I followed her to a house in the forest. The man from the *Beluga* was there. His name is Saran Tuho, isn't it?'

Polus said nothing.

He looked up. It was Jay.

'I tried to catch him,' Jay said, 'but he escaped. It's strange, Polus. I think that you know about this illegal, Saran Tuho. You know about the family that is protecting him and his friends, don't you?'

Polus did not say anything.

Jay laughed. 'It doesn't matter,' he said. I don't have to tell Deva, unless —'

'Unless what?' Polus asked nervously. His mouth was dry.

'Deva is going to retire soon, isn't he?' Jay said. He smiled. 'He likes you. I think that he wants you to be the next Head of the Immigration Department. You must say "no". You must say that I would be a better Head of the Department. Then I will forget everything that I saw yesterday.'

This was blackmail. Polus looked at Jay. Then he noticed a mark on the side of Jay's head. The mark was the size of a small egg.

'What happened to your head?' Polus asked. Jay stopped smiling.

'I had an accident,' Jay replied. 'Think about what I said, Polus.' He got up quickly and left. And he did not pay for his coffee.

9

The Camp in the Forest

On Sunday morning, Jansh was strong enough to get out of bed. Selina was happy. Polus did not want to tell her about his meeting with Jay. He did not want her to be unhappy. But he was very worried.

'What can I do?' he thought. 'What *can* I do? If I'm offered Deva's job, I'll have to say "no". And Jay will be promoted. Then I'll have to leave. I can't take orders from Jay. He's a hard man. And he's not honest. But I can't arrest those men and take them to prison. Myra saved Jansh's life. If Jay or Deva find out that Lisa gave me money, I'll lose my job immediately. I must take it back. That is the first thing to do.'

His son came into the room. They played together for a few minutes.

'I'm going to see Myra's family,' he told his wife. 'I have to speak to them.'

'Can't you go later?' Selina asked. 'Jansh wants to play with you.'

'I know. But I must go now,' he answered. He went out of the house.

Polus found a taxi and drove to the forest.

'I wanted to give those men a chance and Lisa loves that man, Saran,' he thought. 'Jay would never give them a chance. He is a dishonest and violent man. He would not be a good Head of the Immigration Department. I can't work with him if he becomes the new boss. But, if I leave my job, how will I feed my family? Oh! Why didn't I tell Deva everything at the beginning?'

Polus arrived at the house in the forest and Joseph invited him in. Myra was preparing a meal.

'You are welcome here,' said Joseph. 'But why did you come?'

'Myra,' Polus said. 'I want to thank you. You saved my son. Yesterday I couldn't find a doctor to come to my house. You saved Jansh's life.' Myra smiled.

'There is something else,' Polus continued. 'Another immigration officer came here yesterday. His name is Jay.'

'Yes, he came while Saran was here,' said Joseph. 'He tried to catch Saran, but Lisa stopped him. She hit him with a stone from her catapult!'

'So that was his "accident"!' Polus thought. 'Lisa was very brave!'

'I'm afraid that Lisa made things worse,' Myra said. 'The officer took things from us. He said that he will come back for more. Perhaps if we give him money, he will leave us alone.'

'No,' Polus said. 'He will bring police officers and they will search for your friends in the forest. He wants to be the Head of the Immigration Department. I must speak to Saran Tuho. I don't know what I can do, but I want to help.'

'I will take you to him,' Joseph said.

———

Polus and Joseph walked into the forest. The track was

narrow and muddy. Later they came to a river. They walked along the edge of the river for an hour.

Suddenly Joseph stopped. He whistled loudly. Polus heard another whistle somewhere nearby.

A few minutes later, two young men appeared. They smiled when they saw Joseph.

'Who is this man?' one of the men asked.

'He wants to see Saran. It's all right,' Joseph said.

'Follow us,' one of the men replied.

Polus and Joseph followed. They came to some huts made of logs, cut from the trees. This was Saran Tuho's secret camp.

There were about thirty people in the camp – young men and older men. Polus knew some of their faces. He had seen them on the *Beluga*. Some food was cooking in a pot over a fire.

'They have made a good camp,' Polus said to Joseph.

'Yes, but it's difficult here. And soon the rains will come. Then it will be hard to live in this forest,' Joseph said. 'We help them when we can. And they catch animals in the forest and fish in the rivers. A few of the men go into Port Luck to find work. They work on construction sites, but the jobs are dangerous. Nobody checks your ID card on construction sites.'

Polus saw Saran with Lisa. They were sitting together on a log.

Saran got up and came over to Polus and Joseph.

'Have you come to arrest us?' Saran asked.

Polus saw Saran with Lisa.

10

'We're All in Danger'

Everybody in the group was suddenly quiet.

'No, I haven't come to arrest you,' Polus replied.

'Then why are you here?' Saran asked.

'I want to help you. You must go back to Port Luck,' Polus said.

'You say that you want to help us,' Saran said. 'But if we go to Port Luck, you will send us back to the Zipa Islands.'

'I know that you're poor and that you need work,' Polus said. 'But the immigration laws in this country are strict.'

'We need work. There is work here.'

'That's true. But there are some people on Suba who don't like foreigners. The government wants to keep jobs for the people of Suba.' Polus stopped for a moment. Some of the men began to talk to each other.

'I didn't tell my boss that you were in the forest,' Polus went on. 'I wanted to give you a chance. I waited too long. Now Jay, the other immigration officer, knows that you're here. He will bring police to find you. They will catch you and send you back to Zipa.'

'They will never find us. We can hide in this forest,' Saran said. 'We'll never go back to Zipa.'

'Can you run and hide all your lives?' Polus asked. 'If you come back with me, I'll try to help you. It's your only chance. But first you must all go back to the jail in Port Luck. You must trust me. Myra saved my son's life. I can't forget that. I will speak to my boss – Mr Deva. Perhaps his boss in Ranamena, the Chief of Police and Immigration, will let you stay.'

'I have to talk to the others,' Saran said. 'We have to decide together.' He shouted to the other men.

The men came and sat in a circle. Saran spoke, then they all talked at once. An older man raised his hand, and everyone was silent. The man spoke slowly for a few minutes. Polus waited patiently. A light wind started to move the tops of the trees. At last, Saran stood up and came back to Polus.

'We can't agree,' he told Polus. 'I trust you, but the others are not sure. And there is something else. The old man who spoke is my father. He says that a typhoon is coming. We're all in danger.'

'What do you mean?' Polus asked. 'Typhoons never come to Suba.'

'My father understands the winds and the weather,' Saran replied. 'The Zipa Islands often have typhoons. He says that Port Luck is in danger.'

Again the trees moved from side to side. The wind was a little stronger now.

Polus shook his head. 'I don't believe it,' he said.

'Go back home now,' Saran said. 'We will decide soon. We understand the choice that we have. We go back to the jail in Port Luck and you will try to help us. Or Jay will send the police to find us.'

Joseph and Polus walked back to Joseph's house. 'I must see Deva,' Polus thought. 'He's the only person who can

help now. If he doesn't help, then there is no hope for
these men.'

11

A Telephone Call

The Chief of Police and Immigration picked up the phone.
He was in his office in Ranamena, the main city of Suba.

'Chief,' a voice said, 'there's a problem here in Port
Luck. There's an immigration officer here who is helping
illegal workers. He's helping them to get ID cards and
work papers. The illegals are hiding in the forest. The
officer visits them —'

'Who am I talking to?' the Chief asked.

'This is Immigration Officer Jay,' the voice answered.

'And who is helping these illegals?' the Chief asked.

'His name is Polus,' the voice answered.

'Is there anyone else?' the Chief asked.

'I'm not sure. But Polus is a good friend of Deva.'

'Thank you, Officer Jay.'

The Chief of Police and Immigration put his phone
down.

'Deva!' the Chief thought. 'I understand now. He never
catches these illegals. So that is what is going on. The
illegals pay the immigration officers in Port Luck. Then
the illegals get their papers. I'll stop that.'

He picked up the phone and called the Immigration

office in Port Luck.

'Is that Deva?' the Chief asked.

'Yes, is that you, Chief?'

'Yes, Deva. Come over to Ranamena, to my office. Right now.'

'What's it about, Chief?' said Deva.

'Illegal workers.'

The Chief put the telephone down.

Deva left his office to go to the office of the Chief of Police and Immigration.

'This means trouble,' he thought.

Half an hour later, Deva arrived at the Chief's office in Ranamena. He went in and sat down.

'Deva, you never catch any illegal workers,' the Chief said in a hard voice. 'Now I know why.'

'That's not true,' Deva replied. 'We do catch some. But it's not easy —'

'Deva,' the Chief said angrily. 'One of your officers is helping these illegals.'

'Who?' asked Deva. He was surprised.

'An officer called Polus,' said the Chief. 'And I believe he's taking money from these illegals.'

'Polus? No, never!' Deva cried. 'He's a good man and a good officer. Who reported this?'

'It was Officer Jay who reported this,' the Chief said. 'Deva, has Officer Polus told you that a group of illegals are hiding in the forest?'

'Some illegals escaped from jail in Port Luck last week, sir,' Deva replied. 'We know that they're in the forest, but we don't know where. As you know, the forest is very large, more than a thousand square kilometres.'

'Has Polus told you that *he* knows where the illegals are? Has he told you that he has visited them in the forest?'

There was a silence in the room. Outside, the wind began to blow more strongly.

At last the Chief spoke.

'I will send some men to arrest Officer Polus and take him to Port Luck jail,' he said.

An hour later, four police officers with guns knocked at the door of Polus' house. Polus was at home. He opened the door.

'Good day, Polus,' one of the men said. 'You have been helping illegals. We have official papers here – an arrest warrant. You're under arrest. Please come with us.'

12

More Arrests

At seven o'clock the next morning, a loud bell rang in the main police building in Port Luck. Minutes later, all the officers were outside in the yard. They all stood in line. The Chief of Police and Immigration came into the yard. Officer Jay was walking beside him. The sky above was dark and a strong wind was blowing.

'Men,' the Chief said in his strong, sharp voice, 'thirty illegal immigrants escaped from jail in Port Luck last week. They're now hiding in a camp in the forest with their leader, Saran Tuho. We have to catch them quickly. The government wants to send them back to their homes in the Zipa Islands. We have too many illegal immigrants in Suba. Officer Jay knows where the illegals are. He will be in charge. He will give you your instructions. Take jeeps and a truck. You'll need guns and dogs. We must catch these illegals before they leave their camp and go further into the forest. Any questions?'

'Sir,' one of the officers said. 'A storm is coming. Rains will make it difficult to travel in the forest.'

'OK,' the Chief said sharply. 'You must leave now. I want those illegals in Port Luck jail tomorrow.'

The Chief turned and walked back to his office. Outside in the yard, the police officers made preparations. Jay gave his orders. At last he was in charge!

Four jeeps and a truck went along the main street of Port Luck. There were four men in each jeep. Jay sat beside the driver of the first jeep. The jeeps and the truck went along the road out of Port Luck towards the forest. Rain began to fall.

After some time, Jay spoke to the driver of the first jeep.

'You're coming to a fork in the road,' Jay said. 'Take the road on the right.'

The jeeps and the truck went on through the forest. The rain was heavier now and soon there was mud on the road. The mud got deeper. The vehicles went on slowly. Jay became impatient.

'Come on,' he said to his driver. 'Can't you go faster? We'll never get there. We'll never catch these men.'

Jay's driver tried to go faster. But suddenly the jeep sank into the mud and fell on one side. The second jeep came and pulled the first jeep out of the mud. The vehicles went on again but soon it was impossible to go further.

'Get out of the vehicles,' Jay ordered. 'We must find these illegals.'

The police officers began to walk. Soon their uniforms were covered in mud. They slipped and sank into the mud. At last, they came to Joseph's house. They opened the door and went in. Joseph, Myra and Lisa were there.

'You are under arrest!' Jay shouted.

Joseph looked at Jay calmly.

'Where is the arrest warrant?' he asked.

'We don't need an arrest warrant,' Jay shouted. 'You are

The jeep sank into the mud and fell on one side.

hiding illegal workers.'

'But we are citizens of Suba,' Joseph replied. 'Look.'

He showed Jay some papers.

'These are my ID papers,' Joseph said. 'You cannot arrest us without a warrant.'

'Yes, I can arrest you,' Jay cried. 'Put them in the truck,' Jay ordered his men. He took the ID papers from Joseph.

The officers held Joseph, Myra and Lisa. They took them to the jeeps.

The police officers, Jay and their prisoners went slowly back to Port Luck. The wind and rain were stronger now. At last, they got back to Port Luck. Jay went to the Chief of Police and Immigration.

'We have arrested three people, sir,' he said. 'They are a family that is hiding the illegals. The others escaped in the forest.'

'Only three?' the Chief said. 'Let me see their papers.'

Jay gave the ID papers to the Chief.

The Chief looked at them carefully. 'These are legal ID papers, officer,' he said. 'These people are citizens of Suba. And you can't prove that they're hiding illegal immigrants.'

'Sir, I can prove it. I need more time. I know where the illegals are hiding,' Jay replied nervously. 'And your men can question these people. They will soon get the answers that they need!'

'Officer Jay,' the Chief answered. His voice was angry. 'You said, "I know where these illegals are hiding. I can find them." ' His face was red. He stopped for a moment.

Then he went on, 'You were in charge. You had to find thirty illegals from the *Beluga*. And you didn't find them. You have failed. OK, take these three people to jail now. We'll question them again tomorrow.'

'Failed!' Jay thought angrily. 'I haven't failed. I'll get those illegals.' But he said nothing to the Chief. He went away. Then he had an idea.

13

The Typhoon

The rain fell for hour after hour. Soon the roads were rivers, the fields were lakes and the rivers were seas of muddy, brown water. Everywhere, the water rose higher and higher.

Polus was in a cell in Port Luck jail. The water came under the door of his cell. The water began to rise inside his cell.

'If the water rises more, I'm going to drown,' he thought.

He knocked hard on the door. 'Let me out!' he shouted. 'Let me out!'

Suddenly, a small window in the door of the cell opened. It was Jay. He had a smile on his face.

'Jay!' Polus said angrily. 'What did you say to the police, Jay? Why am I in this jail? My wife and child are alone in this terrible storm!'

'It was a mistake,' said Jay coldly. 'You will soon be free. The guard will let you out. And your friends can come out of the forest. The Chief says that they can stay in Suba.'

Jay turned and went. He got into a jeep and drove away.

————

'Can I trust Jay?' Polus thought. 'Is he telling the truth? Will the guard come and let me out? What can I do? My wife and son are in danger in this storm. And I'll die if I stay in this cell. I'll have to trust him. I have no choice.'

At last, a guard came and opened the cell door. Polus ran out of the cell. In the jail yard, he saw Joseph and Myra.

'We're free!' said Polus. 'And the Chief of Police and Immigration says that Saran and his men can stay in Suba.'

'Are you sure?' Joseph asked.

'If it's true, that's wonderful news,' Myra said.

'But where is Lisa?' Polus asked.

Suddenly there was a great crash. The wind was blowing very strongly now. Trees broke and crashed to the ground. Doors and windows broke. Electricity lines came down.

'We can't leave now,' Joseph said. 'It is too dangerous. This is a strong building. It is safe here.'

'You're right,' Polus answered. 'But we can't stay in the cells. They are filling with water. Let's try to find the guard room. It's sure to be strong and safe.'

The wind was so strong that it was difficult to get to the

Suddenly there was a great crash.

guard room.

'I hope that Selina and Jansh are OK,' Polus thought.

———

Polus, Myra and Joseph did not sleep that night. At last, in the early morning of the next day, the terrible winds and rain began to stop. The typhoon moved slowly away from Port Luck.

In the morning light, they saw trees and pieces of wood, mud and water, bricks and glass everywhere.

Then Polus saw Deva coming into the jail yard. There were some men with him. One of them was Saran Tuho!

'Polus, are you all right?' Deva asked. 'I'm sorry that you're here. The Chief gave the order for your arrest. It was a mistake.'

'That's what Jay told me,' Polus said. 'Jay said that I was free now. But where is he?'

'I think that he has gone to the forest to look for the illegals. But he's crazy to go in this weather,' Deva said.

'Polus,' Saran said. 'The people of Port Luck need help – quickly. In the Zipa Islands we know about typhoons. We have come to help.'

14

After the Storm

Polus, Saran and his men worked for many hours. Then Polus went home. 'I must see if Selina and Jansh are safe,' he thought.

When he got home, he found that there was a big hole in the roof of his house and that the windows were all broken. The door was open. But his wife was still there.

'Oh! Polus!' Selina cried. 'I'm so pleased to see you. Are you all right?'

'Yes,' he answered. 'And you – and Jansh?'

'Yes, we're OK,' Selina said. 'Oh, I'm so pleased to see you, Polus.'

'But I have to go again now,' Polus said. 'I have to help the people of Port Luck.'

He went back to find Saran and the other men. They worked all night. They found people in the broken shops and houses – some were alive, some were dead.

The next day, everyone was very, very tired. But they had to keep working. There was so much to do.

Deva came to see Polus. 'Jay has disappeared. I have spoken to the Chief. He understands everything now. He has sent some men to find Jay. They are going to arrest him.'

Polus was tired and worried when he went home that night. He walked up the muddy street, to his house. He went inside. Selina and Jansh were in the living-room. Suddenly, someone pushed Polus from behind. He fell onto the floor.

'Get up!' It was Jay's voice.

Polus got up slowly.

'What do you want?' asked Polus.

Jay's face and uniform were muddy and he had a crazy

look in his eyes. There was a gun in his hand and he was pointing it at Polus.

'I wanted to be the next Head of Immigration. I wanted to be in charge. Now the police are looking for me, and I have to hide like one of those illegals. And it's all because of you, Polus!'

'No, Jay. You know that's not true.'

'Shut up or I'll kill you. Perhaps I'll kill you later. But now I think that I'll take your son with me. Don't try to follow me, or I'll kill him!'

'No!' Selina cried.

Jay stepped forward and picked up Jansh. He went out of the door and onto the street. Polus ran forward. He heard a sharp *crack*. And then Jay fell slowly to the ground.

Jansh ran back to the house. 'Mummy!' he cried.

Polus went to look at Jay. He picked up Jay's gun. A stone the size of a small egg lay nearby. Somebody with a catapult came from behind a tree. It was Lisa.

15

'I Want to Thank You'

A week later Port Luck had electricity and water again.

'These people from the Zipa Islands are good people,' the Chief of Police and Immigration thought. 'They have worked hard – very hard.'

He picked up the phone and called the Minister of the

Jay stepped forward and picked up Jansh.

Interior.

'I hear that you have done a wonderful job in Port Luck,' the Minister said. 'Well done.'

'Yes,' the Chief of Police and Immigration answered. 'And we have to thank a group of illegal workers from the Zipa Islands. They and their leader, a man called Saran Tuho, saved many lives. They're wonderful workers. Our country needs people like them.'

'What are you saying?' the Minister asked.

'Well,' the Chief answered. 'Perhaps we can give them official work papers. Perhaps we can give them legal IDs. What do you think?'

'I'm not sure,' the Minister replied, 'I'll have to think.'

Later the Minister phoned the Chief of Police and Immigration.

'OK,' he said. 'We'll give the illegals their work papers.'

———

Saran Tuho and all the men from the *Beluga* were in the yard of the main police building in Port Luck. The Chief of Police and Immigration, Deva, Polus, Selina, Jansh, Myra and Lisa were all there.

'Saran Tuho,' the Chief said. 'I want to thank you and your people for helping us. You have had difficult times, but you have saved the lives of many people from Suba. I have spoken to the Minister of the Interior. He says that you are all welcome in our country. You can stay here. You can go to the Immigration office for your papers tomorrow.'

Then the Chief spoke to Polus quietly.

'I was wrong,' he said. 'Suba needs people like these. There is a lot of work here. We must help our neighbours.'

'As they helped us,' Polus said.

Saran was holding Lisa's hand. The two young people came over to Polus.

'Thank you,' Lisa said. 'The people of Suba will be proud of you.'

Polus smiled. Then he turned and walked home.

Points for Understanding

1

1 Why were Polus and Jay waiting for the *Beluga*?
2 What did they find at first in the ship's hold?
3 What did the ship's captain offer the two immigration officers?
4 How many illegal immigrants were there?
5 What did one of the illegal immigrants do?

2

1 What did Deva tell Polus?
2 How had the prisoners escaped?
3 What did Deva want to do?
4 What did Rosa think was wrong with the ID papers?

3

1 Who did Polus see in a grey truck?
2 What did Polus do then?
3 What was the problem with the taxi?
4 Who helped Polus?
5 Who was inside the house?
6 What was on the table?
7 What was Lisa doing?
8 Why did Lisa get up and run out of the room?

4

1 Where did Lisa and Myra come from?
2 What has happened in the last two years?
3 What had Polus left at Joseph's house?
4 What was wrong with Jansh?
5 Why could Polus not sleep?
6 What did Polus want for his family?

5

1 Who saw Polus get into a taxi?
2 Who came to the office?
3 What did she give Polus?
4 What did she ask Polus to do?
5 Why did Selina phone Polus?
6 What can Aunt Myra do?
7 What did Jay find on the floor?

6

1 Who followed Polus?
2 Who knocked on the door of Polus' and Selina's house?
3 Why are siren crabs dangerous?
4 What did Myra give Jansh?
5 What does Polus have to do?
6 Will Jansh get better?

7

1 What did Jay think?
2 Why did Jay fall to the ground?
3 What did Jay take from Joseph and Myra?

8

1 What did Polus find inside his notebook?
2 Who came to sit down with Polus?
3 What did he want Polus to say?

9

1 Why did Polus go back to see Joseph and Myra?
2 Where did Joseph take Polus?
3 What did Saran Tuho ask Polus?

10

1 What did Polus want Saran Tuho and his men to do?
2 Who trusted Polus and who did not?
3 What did Saran Tuho's father say?
4 Who did Polus think could help?

11

1 What did Jay say to the Chief of Police and Immigration?
2 What did the Chief say to Deva?
3 Who did the four police officers arrest?

12

1 Who did the Chief put in charge?
2 Jay's driver tried to go faster. What happened then?
3 Who did Jay and his men arrest?
4 Did they have an arrest warrant?
5 Was the Chief pleased with Jay's work?

13

1 Describe the weather. Use three sentences.
2 Who opened the window in the door of Polus' cell?
3 Jay said, 'The Chief says that Saran Tuho and his
   men can stay in Suba.' Was this true?
4 Why did Saran Tuho and his men come to Port Luck?

14

1 How long did Saran Tuho and his men work?
2 Who did Jay take from Polus' house?
3 What happened to Jay when he went out of the door?

15

1 What did the Chief of Police and Immigration ask the Minister?
2 What did the Chief say to Saran Tuho and his men?
3 What did Lisa say to Polus?

Macmillan Heinemann English Language Teaching
Between Towns Road, Oxford
A division of Macmillan Publishers Limited of Brunel Rd,
Houndmills, Basingstoke, Hampshire RG21 6XS
Companies and representatives throughout the world

ISBN 0 435 27302 7

Text © Roderick Neilsen 1999
Design and illustration © Macmillan Publishers Limited England 1999

Heinemann is a registered trademark of Reed Educational & Professional Publishing Limited

First published 1999

All rights reserved; no part of this publication may be reproduced,
stored in a retrieval system, transmitted in any form, or by any means,
electronic, mechanical, photocopying, recording, or otherwise, without
the prior written permission of the publishers.

*This is a work of fiction. Any similarities to people, institutions, corporations
or public bodies bearing the same name are purely coincidental.*

Editorial development by Phoenix Publishing Services
Illustrated by Martin Salisbury
Typography by Adrian Hodgkins
Designed by Sue Vaudin
Cover by Alex Williamson and Marketplace Design
Typeset in 11.5/14.5pt Goudy
Printed and bound in Spain

2003 2002 2001 2000 1999
10 9 8 7 6 5 4 3 2 1